Victoria and Albert Museum

Getting Dressed

The Arts and Living

Edward T Joy

General editors for the series John Fleming and Hugh Honour

D1166946

London: Her Majesty's Stationery Office

With the following exception all the objects
illustrated are from the Victoria and Albert
Museum.
Fig.1 British Museum.

Design by HMSO Graphic Design

ISBN 0 11 290285 5

Contents

Preface

Compressing all the information about getting dressed into my allotted space reminds one of the intricacies of a Sheraton dressing table: so much has to go into so little. The very contents of the dressing table, to say nothing of what stands upon it when, as Pope wrote, 'unveil'd the Toilet stands displayed', could absorb a whole volume. Fortunately the guide lines are laid down, so that the Museum's fascinating collection of the furniture used over the last three centuries by women and men (the latter must never be forgotten) in the task of preparing themselves properly for company, can be seen and enjoyed by all.

My thanks are due to Mr. J. Fleming for first showing me the way, and to Mr. T. M. MacRobert for helping me to illustrate it.

Edward T. Joy.

1 Introduction

A frequent theme in literature throughout the world is the inordinate time women have taken to complete their dressing with its accompanying attention to arranging the hair and applying cosmetics. This has been variously the subject of ironical comment, ridicule, rebuke or outright condemnation, according to the standpoint of the commentator and the mood of the times. It is, of course, grossly unfair to pick out women for such comment as men have taken just as long over their toilet preparations and have been equally adept in the use of cosmetics and perfumes. Painted adornment for the face and body and intricate hair styles have always had universal significance both in time and place, shared from antiquity to the present equally by fashionable society in advanced civilisations and by primitive and savage tribes.

Archaeology bears this out before literary evidence is available. The Etruscans have left mirrors, boxes for unguents and jars for perfumes. The Assyrians, like the Egyptians, had elaborate hair styles which were of formal social significance in court etiquette. When Ovid's *Ars Amatoria* (1st century A.D.) and Vatsayana's *Kama Sutra* (probably between first and sixth century A.D.) refer to the use of cosmetics in, respectively, imperial Rome and India, they deal with long-established practices equally applicable to the woad of the ancient Britons and the body colouring and tattooing of the early barbarian invaders of Britain, the Saxons and Norsemen.

Toilet preparations require their necessary equipment. In the British Museum there is a small but intricately arranged toilet box of about 1300 B.C. which belonged to a noble lady of ancient Egypt. It is fitted for a variety of cosmetics including eye pencils and three pots which, though now empty, once held perfumed ointments and face creams. Other contents are a bronze dish for mixing colours for make-up, and pumice stone for removing body hair and smoothing rough skin. Perhaps of even greater interest are the articles proving the leisurely business of preparation–a pair of comfortable slippers for indoor use (the outdoor sandals are also in the box) and pads or small cushions for supporting the elbows while the cosmetics are carefully applied.

Perfumes, cosmetics and hair dyes, inherited mainly from Egypt, were used by the Greeks and earned Plato's censure. In the Roman world [fig.1], where luxury reached new proportions and cosmetics were in even wider use, among men as well as women, writers were divided into two camps; Lucretius, Martial and Juvenal poured scorn on such practices while Ovid, who wrote of false eyebrows, eye shadow, wigs and patches, was very much in their favour.

Figure 1. Woman at her toilet, later Roman period, early 3rd century A.D.

The early Christian Church frowned on personal adornment as it did on self-indulgence generally. Painting the face was the licentious custom of the degenerate ancient world and was not Jezebel, who 'painted her face and tired her head'–the only reference in the Old Testament to the use of cosmetics–the most abandoned woman in the Bible?

By the end of the Middle Ages the Renaissance and the opening up of new trade routes changed the situation drastically. Venice was to set the standard for Tudor England. She imported perfumes from the East (Lady Macbeth's 'all the perfumes of Arabia'). Venetian ceruse, a revival of the ancient mixture of white lead and vinegar, which provided the skin with its admired whiteness and at the same time was highly dangerous, was to be in universal use for two centuries. From France came Hungary water (originally a gift to the French king), distilled water of rosemary flowers in spirits of wine, to be used as widely as eau-de-cologne was to be later. 'Spanish rouge', with a base of ochre, was rated the best in the fashionable world.

2 England to 1660

As for England, in the poem *The Romaunt of the Rose*, written in the late fourteenth century and attributed to Chaucer though probably only partly written by him, Idleness appears in the person of a fashionable young woman of the time. She has yellow hair, plucked eyebrows ('smooth and slick'), a little mouth and white face and throat. She 'had in hand a gay mirror'. Here, dressing equipment begins to take shape, for central to all the preparations for dressing, doing one's hair and putting on cosmetics, and thus central to the arrangement of furniture connected with these activities, is the mirror, the dressing-, looking- and toilet-glass as it is also called. Mirrors made from various materials have a very long history but surviving English toilet-glasses date only from the late seventeenth century. In medieval times small hand mirrors, the equivalent of modern handbag compacts, were usually carried hanging from the girdle or in specially made cases, and were regarded as jewellery. As such they hardly come within the category of domestic furniture, but they must often have stood upon tables or similar pieces when in the house. Burnished metal, glass or crystal were the usual materials. Rock crystal, a variety of quartz, was particularly prized as it was in many ways superior to glass; it was harder, polished better and did not blur or cloud with time. It is not surprising that when the famous clear Venetian glass was produced in the early sixteenth century it was called crystal glass. Some early mirrors were described as made of burnished steel–a misleading term as this was not steel in the modern sense but another name for speculum, a silvery-white alloy which could take a high polish. It was very heavy so that steel mirrors, like indeed most mirrors of the time, were small in size.

Hanging mirrors were introduced into England in the fifteenth century. By the early Tudor period there are references to 'standing glasses' to rest on a table or other suitable piece of furniture, but small hand mirrors remained in general use among the well-to-do for dressing. Queen Elizabeth I is known to have had a considerable number of these, made of metal or crystal. Other monarchs, according to royal inventories, had both standing and hand mirrors–Charles I, for instance, had a standing mirror in a silver gilt frame which was sold for £21 after his execution–but their description is too vague to determine their exact character. Sir Robert Mansell established the first English glass factory in 1618 and produced the first English looking-glasses, but none has survived and there is no evidence of the numbers that were produced or even of what they looked like.

The use of cosmetics became widespread in Elizabeth's reign, inspired by the Queen's example. Paints, salves, patches, pomanders with perfumes of many kinds, hair dyes and wigs, used by men and women alike, spread down from fashionable society to the rising middle class. Already in 1548 Bishop Hooper complained that 'even the forty shilling a year man will waste his morning time while he sets his beard in order.' Later the 'Italianate Englishman' dyed his beard to match the colour of the Queen's hair and wore perfumed gloves. As for women, Hamlet railed at Ophelia, 'I have heard of your painting too, well enough; God has given you one face and you make yourselves another.' Naturally severest criticism came from the Puritans, particularly from their chief pamphleteer, Philip Stubbes. Of women who painted their faces he wrote (*Anatomie of Abuses*, 1583): 'Do they think thus to adulterate the Lord his workmanship and to be without offence?' Looking-glasses were 'the devil's bellows, wherewith he bloweth the blast of pride in our hearts.'

Pomanders, the ancestors of scent bottles, were containers filled with aromatic essences which the well-to-do used to carry with them as a guard against infection. These pomanders were themselves versions of the medieval musk balls, shaped like an apple or orange, which were carried in the hand or hung from the neck or waist. When Cardinal Wolsey went in stately procession to Westminster Hall, so we are told by his gentleman usher and biographer, George Cavendish, he used to hold to his nose 'against the pestilent airs' an orange with its inside extracted and replaced by a sponge soaked in vinegar. This orange shape, in gold or silver, its inside divided into sections attached to a central core, was fashionable in the sixteenth and seventeenth centuries until supplanted by scent bottles.

But in spite of this abundant evidence in the Tudor and early Stuart periods of the use of cosmetics and of the growing variety of receptacles needed to contain them, there is no clear indication of the kind of tables which were required to hold them and the many additional accessories such as brushes, combs and glasses. Contemporary inventories of bedroom furniture mention wainscot tables covered with a carpet or cloth and it is likely that these served as dressing tables. Such tables would no doubt also have drawers and indeed an early record of 'dressing tables with drawers' occurs in the household expenses of Sir Edward Dering in 1652. But it is not until after the Restoration of Charles II in 1660 that distinct types of dressing tables can be identified with certainty. During the Puritan rule of the Commonwealth (1649–60) the use of cosmetics and expensive dressing equipment was frowned upon, although the diarist John Evelyn notes on 11 May, 1654, 'women began to paint themselves again, formerly a most ignominious thing, and used only by prostitutes.'

For storing clothes various pieces of furniture–chests and cupboards of all kinds–were in use in early times, but we are here concerned with the clothes press, known now as the wardrobe, which has become the main storage piece in bedroom suites. Chests were the most important storage receptacles for wearing apparel in the Middle Ages when monarchs and feudal magnates regularly took their furniture with them on the tours of their territories. When furniture lost this nomadic character the chest retained its use for storage and gradually became the chest of drawers. Cupboards pose a problem, for until the Tudor period they were open shelved structures (cup-boards). Early enclosed pieces were usually known as aumbries or presses. By about 1625, however, close or joined cupboards for clothes became plentiful in the great Elizabethan and Jacobean houses and thus the clothes-press had clearly succeeded the chest as the principal storage piece. The fashionable padded trunk and hose, doublets and the wide farthingale dresses were hung in these presses many of which have retained their original wooden pegs. Smaller articles, such as hats and ruffs, were kept in chests or in the drawers which were often found at the base of the clothes press.

Figure 2 is a good example of about 1620. Of oak, it has two panelled doors in the upper part and a drawer in the lower. There is typical Jacobean ornament in the strapwork on the cornice, fluting on the uprights and lunettes on the lower rail. This form was to persist among country craftsmen until a much later date, apart from changes in decoration and construction. By 1650, for example, architectural features appear on surviving examples–moulded arches on the panels, and cornices, dentils and trusses on the uprights.

Figure 2.
Oak panelled
clothes press,
c.1620.

11

3 The Later Stuarts 1660-1714

From the late Stuart period changes in the character of fashionable costume led to alterations in the interior arrangement of clothes presses. Thinner and lighter materials were in use; clothes were no longer hung from pegs but were folded flat and laid on sliding shelves or in drawers. Even when hooped costume was worn by ladies the hoop itself was removable and dresses were folded for storage. Thus presses still kept their established form but now had a series of shelves or trays in the upper part.

The original meaning of the word 'toilet' was the cloth or cover on the table used for dressing accessories. In the later Stuart period the meaning was being transferred from the cover to the accessories themselves. An early example of this change, at a time when both meanings were in use, is found in the entry in Evelyn's diary for 9 June, 1662 when, on a visit to Hampton Court to see the new Queen, Catherine of Braganza, shortly after her marriage to Charles II, he noticed 'the great looking-glass and toilet, of beaten and massive gold, given by the Queen-Mother'.

After the Restoration some fine silver toilet sets were made. The looking-glass was supported by a strut and the accessories included a variety of boxes, scent-canisters, combs, etc [pls.1, 2]. In a set in the Victoria and Albert Museum the mirror frame is elaborately embossed with flowers, foliage, amorini and acanthus. Its crest bears a medallion decorated in low relief with human figures and surrounded by swirls of foliage. The set includes a pair of salvers on feet, a pair of oblong caskets, two pairs of round boxes, a pair of two-handled covered bowls, a pair of small covered vases and a pin-cushion, all stamped with the maker's mark 'WF' and the London hall-mark of 1683–4 [pl.3, fig.3].

Figure 3. Toilet set of embossed silver, London, 1683–4.

No fashionable dressing table was now complete without its patch box. The wearing of dark-coloured patches on a whitened skin had already a very long history; the ancient Romans wore them as they resembled moles which were regarded, strangely enough, as marks of beauty, in sharp contrast to the more recent purpose of hiding blemishes on the skin. The practice, revived in the sixteenth century, spread rapidly throughout Europe and reached its heyday for perhaps half a century after 1660. Usually a small black circular patch was favoured, but there were many other shapes, some of them relatively simple, such as stars and crescents, other extremely fanciful; we hear, for instance, of birds, trees and even a coach and horses. The required shape was cut from black velvet, taffeta or silk and sometimes from Spanish leather, and attached by mastic to the face, throat and breast. Samuel Pepys, the other celebrated diarist of the Restoration, mentions the custom several times. His wife first wore black patches in August, 1660. On 26 April, 1667, he describes Lady Newcastle, whose extravagance was the talk of the town, as wearing 'many black patches because of pimples about her mouth'. The fashion was by no means confined to ladies; men also frequently wore them, even, it is said, to indicate their political leanings, Whigs wearing them on the right cheek, Tories on the left. Patches were kept in special patch boxes, round or oval in shape, about two inches across, made of tortoiseshell, silver or, later, the famous Battersea enamel on brass. The boxes usually had a small mirror or a disc of polished steel inside the lid.

Fashionable ladies and gentlemen now often received their intimate friends while completing their toilet at their dressing tables *[pl.4]*. Tradespeople were also frequently in attendance. In Sir John Vanbrugh's well-known play, *The Relapse*, first produced in 1696, Lord Foppington is attended in his dressing room not only by his servant and a page, and by his brother (who has his own servant with him), but also by his shoemaker, tailor, hosier, sempstress and barber (who is his periwig-maker). Many of these tables, as contemporary illustrations show, were completely covered with draperies and this was to be a familar feature until the end of the Georgian period and beyond. There were also varieties of knee-hole tables without draperies which came into fashion in the later seventeenth century and which, subject to modifications in style, ornament and material, have never disappeared from dressing rooms and bedrooms. These early tables had a simple elegance. They were usually veneered with walnut and at first stood on turned straight legs joined by curved stretchers, then, after about 1700, on cabriole legs without stretchers. It was on this type of table that the swing toilet glasses on box stands normally stood. Above and on either side of the knee-hole were drawers for combs, brushes and the numerous cosmetics. In the early eighteenth century dressing tables were often veneered with a variety of woods or decorated with japanning or gilt gesso. When, about 1725, the introdution of mahogany led to a revival of carved ornament, the cabriole legs were often decorated with carved acanthus on the knee pieces and ended on carved claw-and-ball feet.

Japanning, the English imitation of oriental lacquer, an expensive luxury imported by the East India Company, was much favored by those who could not afford costly decoration. What gave special impetus to the fashion was the publication in 1688 of the popular manual, *A Treatise of Japanning and Varnishing* by John Stalker and George Parker. This contained full instructions, with illustrations, for making japan and for decoration in the Chinese manner. The vogue was taken up by enthusiastic amateurs, for the work could easily be done at home. It was not only furniture that was japanned; the *Treatise* included patterns for decorating powder, patch and comb boxes, brushes, combs and mirrors, for all of which this craze for chinoiserie was considered particularly suitable. Practically all this early japanned work, however, has disappeared for the ingredients proved unsatisfactory for providing permanent bright colours. Nevertheless, japanning was to remain a favourite decoration for bedroom furniture and as techniques improved many later examples have survived.

The knee-hole dressing tables acquired pedestals of drawers or cupboards at each side of the central recess and a drawer above it. They were also used for writing as the bedroom was usually the best place for one's private correspondence. The table top was sometimes hinged and could be raised to reveal a central looking-glass and compartments for the toilet articles, or these could be found in the top drawer. A special writing slide was often found beneath the top, or a writing flap took the place of the looking glass within the table, in which case a toilet glass would stand on the top.

A very fashionable arrangement of furniture in the late Stuart and early Georgian periods was the combination known as 'table, glass and stands', in which the table, standing beneath a looking-glass on the wall, was flanked by a pair of stands to hold candle-sticks. This set could be found in various rooms of the house but it was certainly extensively used in bedrooms. Many sets formed part of the bedroom equipment of royal residences. In 1698 William III's Lord Chamberlain informed the Master of the Great Wardrobe that it was 'His Majesty's pleasure that you give orders for mending the Gilt Table, Glasses and Stands in ye great Bedchamber at Kensington'. In the same year 'a

Table, Glass and Stands' were supplied for His Majesty's Bedchamber at Newmarket. Between 1716 and 1717 the royal furniture-makers, John Gumley and James Moore were paid by the Lord Chamberlain

'For a hanging glass in a walnuttree fframe with a walnuttree Table and a pair of Stands for Madam Kilmansark's Bedchamber and dressing Room and the Baron's Bedchamber at Hampton Court.'[1]

Randle Holme, whose *Academy of Armory,* published in 1688 but written much earlier, is a mine of information about the interior of the house, describes the contents of the bedroom as including 'tables, stands, dressing box with drawers, a large Myrour or Looking glass'. He defines a toilet glass as a square mirror resting on a stay and having a ring also at the top to hang it, and adds: 'these sorts of glasses are most used by Ladys to look their faces in, and to see how to dress their heads and set their top knots on the foreheads upright'. Many of the surviving toilet glasses, from about 1660, have these rings and struts. The frames are decorated in various ways. An early and typically English decoration is stump work, a form of needlework in which the ornament is carried out in relief on a backing of wadding or wool and in which the technical skill of the worker (for this was one of the great ages of English needlework) is combined with quaint and somewhat naive but nonetheless attractive pictorial designs. In the example in figure 4 (p.25) the wooden frame has gilt diaper and floral ornament on black lacquer. Between the glass and the edge of the frame the stump work represents, at the top, a lady under a canopy and two buildings, at the sides a King and Queen, and below a lion and a unicorn. Another form of decoration was filigree work which, like stump work and japanning, had special appeal because it could be done cheaply at home *[fig.5,* p.26*].* Strips of coloured and gilt paper were rolled and twisted to form complex patterns including birds and flowers. Filigree work was sometimes combined with stump work or with a japanned crest and outer frame.

1. Public Record Office. Lord Chamberlain's Accounts, 5/131 (Kensington Palace and Newmarket); 5/47 (Hampton Court).

Plate 1. Silver toilet set from Sizergh Castle, English, 17th century.

Plate 2. Two octagonal boxes from the Sizergh Castle set.

Plate 3. Silver box, part of the set in Plate 1, decorated with probably a Chinese scene.

Plate 4. Marquetry decoration on top of dressing table, 1674.

Plate 5. Toilet-glass decorated with chinoiserie in gold lacquer on green ground, c.1700.

Plate 6 (right). Dressing table, mahogany veneered with satinwood, marquetry in Neo-Classical style, c.1775.

Plate 7. Dressing table, satinwood, marquetry and painted decoration, c.1780.

Glass was exciting general interest, for home production was now assured. The Vauxhall glass works were founded about 1663 by the Duke of Buckingham who held patents for making both plate and mirror glass. These works and other glasshouses which were in the same area became the main source of supply of English glass until the end of the Georgian period. Richard Steele in *The Lover* has left us a graphic account of his visit in 1715 to John Gumley's looking-glass shop in the Strand, convinced that 'we have arrived at such perfection in this ware that it is not in the power of any Potentate in Europe to have so beautiful a mirror as he may purchase here for a trifle.'

The square looking-glass described by Randle Holme was replaced shortly before 1700 by the rectangular upright glass set in a narrower frame with a curved cresting. After about 1700 appeared one of the most attractive of all smaller pieces of English furniture, the toilet-glass of this form mounted on a box stand. The glass was fitted by swivel screws to two slender

Figure 4. Stump work decoration on mirror, late 17th century.

25

Figure 5.
Filigree work on toilet mirror frame, late 17th century.

upright supports. The stand took the form of small drawers or a miniature bureau; in the latter case the long drawer below the writing flap was fitted with small compartments for the toilet materials. Most toilet-glasses of this kind in Queen Anne's reign and shortly afterwards were veneered in plain walnut. Some were veneered with the more expensive burr walnut or with marquetry. Others again were japanned and had oriental decoration to match the general fashion in bedroom furniture; more rare was tortoiseshell decoration. The long bottom drawer, with or without the bureau section, was often of serpentine form. The glass itself, whatever the decoration, was sometimes edged with delicate carved gilt mouldings. Examples are shown in figure 6 and plate 5. A later example, probably made within the decade 1720–30, is veneered with three exotic woods, amboyna, kingwood and rosewood. The swing toilet-glass with curved top stands on a miniature bureau which has three drawers at the side and another three, with concave fronts, below. The supporting table on straight legs has a slide which is hinged in the centre so that it can be folded before being pushed back.

Wardrobes after 1660, for at least some time, were substantially of earlier type. Some had their doors, drawer fronts and sides veneered with walnut and decorated with inlay and crossbanding. Very rarely were they decorated with marquetry; this was reserved for the show pieces in the 'rooms of parade'.

Figure 6. Toilet-glass decorated with burr walnut, c.1700.

4 Georgian Period 1714-1830

Cosmetics in Georgian England were used in ever increasing variety. Gladys Scott Thomson (*The Russells in Bloomsbury 1669–1771*) provides us with a transcription of the bill for cosmetics run up by the young Lady Caroline Russell, daughter of the Duke of Bedford, between 1757 and 1760 (she was still under eighteen in the latter year). The purchases include, in addition to powder, dressing pins, combs, etc., *pomades à baton*, sticks of scented cosmetics for greasing the skin and hair; a swansdown powder puff; a top-knot and tresses of false hair; jars of jasmin pomade; a knife for removing powder; and bear's grease. This bear's grease, an expensive import from France, was literally the animal's fat melted down, scented and used as a basis for creams and rouges. A cheaper substitute, lard, was more usual.

Most of the ingredients of perfumes, dyes, creams, washes and rouges, as well as the finished products, had to be imported from abroad. Already subject to heavy import duties they were made even more costly by a government tax of 1786 which imposed a sliding scale of charges according to their price. Hair powder was further taxed in 1795 when William Pitt, in the stress of the war with France, imposed an annual licence fee of one guinea on all who powdered their hair. The effect was ultimately to end the profuse powdering of women's hair and, in the case of men, to end the long custom of wearing wigs.

Ceruse, commonly called paint, as in 'powder and paint', gave the skin its fashionable whiteness and was also the main ingredient in most rouges and lip salves. Its lead content could be extremely harmful to sensitive skins and could even be fatal. How many women had their complexions ruined and how many were killed off by lead poisoning will never be known. The most celebrated example of its fatal results was Maria Gunning,

Lady Coventry, at one time a noted beauty, who died from this cause in 1760.

Scent bottles on dressing tables were often pear-shaped with flattened sides or oblong, with a short neck; glass was the usual material, clear or coloured, but enamelled copper and gold were also used. An English speciality after about 1753 was the production of porcelain scent bottles, particularly from the Chelsea factory. These had many forms–animals, human figures, birds and fruit–sometimes with their necks, stoppers and bases of gold. Enamelled copper was also used for bottles in imitation of Chelsea porcelain. About 1785 Josiah Wedgwood began to make blue jasperware scent bottles decorated with Neo-Classical ornament in white relief.

Elegance was the keynote of Georgian design and no furniture excelled in that respect the pieces made for dressing. With the publication of Thomas Chippendale's *The Gentleman and Cabinet-Maker's Director* in 1754 the Rococo style, the anglicised version of the French *rocaille*, with its emphasis on C and

Figure 7. Design for a lady's dressing table, plate LII in Chippendale's *Director*, 1762.

S scrolls which were generally carved in mahogany, came into fashion for furniture *[fig.7]*. In the third and enlarged (and also final) edition of the famous pattern book in 1762 there are designs for several varieties of dressing tables which included a lady's dressing table, four 'buroe' dressing tables, two 'dressing chests and bookcase', and two 'toilet tables'. All are of knee-hole type. The lady's dressing table has draperies, complete with fringes and tassels, across the recess which is flanked by pedestal cupboards and has, above, a long drawer fitted with 'all conveniences for dressing' i.e. a mirror 'made to rise' and compartments for combs, rings, bottles, boxes, etc. There is another looking-glass above the table, hinged between two narrow cupboards. Two fine modified versions of this design, one formerly at Kimbolton Castle, the other now in the Lady Lever Art Gallery, have dispensed with the draperies and have drawers fitted at the rear of the knee-hole.

Chippendale's bureau dressing tables are clearly designed with adaptation in mind–and this of course was an avowed aim of his pattern book–for the arrangement is either for a central cupboard at the back of the knee-hole and flanking drawers, or for central drawers and flanking cupboards. Chippendale adds that 'the recess for the knees is a circular form, which looks more handsome than when it is straight'. These bureaux are relatively simple but his other designs, including those with a bookcase above, and his 'toilet tables', are much more elaborate, particularly the latter which have carved ornament and are recommended to be in burnished gold with festoons of draperies.

Among the surviving bills from Chippendale's firm for furniture supplied to Sir Edward Knatchbull at Mersham, Kent, and to Edwin Lascelles at Harewood House, Yorkshire, there is reference to another type of dressing table described as a 'commode chest of drawers'. The Knatchbull accounts, for instance, contain the following entry for 14 October, 1767:

'A large Mahogany Chest of drawers, of fine wood with a dressing drawer complete. £14. 6s.'

Such pieces were chests of drawers with the top (or 'dressing') drawer fitted with the usual compartments, boxes, trays, etc.,

Figure 8. Commode chest of drawers veneered with Cuban mahogany, c.1760.

and this simple and very convenient type was to enjoy a long vogue. An elegant example of about 1760 in the Museum, not connected with Chippendale, is illustrated in figure 8. The drawer fronts are veneered with finely figured Cuban mahogany and the shaped fluted corners, bracket feet and curved apron piece below are decorated with crisply carved Rococo ornament. The whole shows strong French influence.

Early in George III's reign (1760–1820) there was a revival of marquetry just about a century after its general introduction into England, but the decoration now followed the delicate Neo-Classical designs inspired by the interior decoration of the architect Robert Adam. Figure 11 and plate 6 show an example of about 1775. This dressing table is made of mahogany veneered with satinwood and has legs of slender cabriole form; the marquetry, of laburnum, satinwood and various woods, decorates the sides, top and ledge below. The drawer pulls out and the top can be pushed back, disclosing a mirror on a ratchet and two flanking compartments. The lids of the latter are decorated with a male and female bust on a brilliant green ground.

A later and more elaborate example is shown in plate 7. This is made of satinwood, the fashionable wood of the Adam period. The bow shaped front, which contains a dressing drawer, rests on slender turned legs connected by curved stretchers supporting a central box. On the top a nest of five drawers support small cupboards connected by a shield shaped toilet glass. The decoration of garlands is painted and the cupboard doors have grisaille medallions.

In the closing decades of the century English furniture attained, in the words of a distinguished foreign historian (S. Giedion, *Mechanization Takes Command*), a 'restrained mastery' which has given it 'an almost timeless maturity.' Economy of line, allied strictly to function, was now united to elegance by superb craftsmanship and control of decoration *[pl.8 and fig.10]*. The pattern books of Thomas Shearer, George Hepplewhite and Thomas Sheraton excelled in the ingenuity of their fittings for dressing tables. Their designs are interpretations for the middle classes of the Adam style which was the preserve of the wealthy. They were intended to be carried out mainly in mahogany, though other woods were freely advocated. Decoration was varied: inlay, marquetry, painting and japanning. Thomas Shearer, about whom nothing is known, not even his

Figure 9.
Dressing table in Neo-Classical taste (see Pl.9), c.1780.

Figure 10. Pedestal dressing table, c.1775 (see Pl.8).

address, contributed seventeen signed plates, out of a total of twenty, to the first (1788) edition of the *Cabinet-Makers' London Book of Prices,* a trade manual which set out the labour costs of the various pieces of furniture with the object of establishing harmonious trade relations between masters and employees. He was a specialist in dressing tables in several varieties, including 'Rudd's Table'; details of 'Furniture Drawers', i.e. the top drawers of the tables with elaborately fitted and ingeniously planned interiors containing the 'necessary equipage' for dressing and sometimes also for writing; a 'Dressing Stand'; a 'Gentleman's Dressing Stand' of compact nest of drawers form; a 'Gentleman's Round Dressing Table', a bow fronted chest of drawers with a mirror fixed on the inside of the hinged top; and a 'Lady's Dressing Table' of knee-hole form with a swing mirror made to rise outwards at the top from each side.

Hepplewhite was an obscure furniture-maker of Cripplegate, London. Very little is known of his background and no furniture made by him or from his shop has ever been identified. He did

33

Figure 11.
Dressing table,
c.1775 (see Pl.6).

not even live to see the publication of his celebrated pattern book, *The Cabinet-Maker and Upholsterer's Guide*, for it appeared in 1788, two years after his death, and seems to have been issued by his widow *[cf. pl.9 and fig.11]*. Yet the *Guide* has given his name to the distinctive light and delicate furniture which was current in the last quarter of the century. Under his heading of 'Dressing Apparatus' are four designs for ladies' dressing tables, each with the usual compartments 'adapted for combs, powders, essences, pin-cushions and other necessary equipage.' Two of these are of simple table form, the legs united by a broad shelf. A third has chest of drawers form; a fourth is a knee-hole with two small drawers at the sides. The tops of these tables are either hinged at the back so as to open upwards, or are folded to open outwards. 'Dressing Drawers' are standard chests of drawers with their top drawer fitted for dressing requisites. For these, again, four designs are submitted; two are straight fronted and have bracket feet, one of them with a writing slide; the other two have shaped fronts, one serpentine the other bow, both with the delicate outward-curving feet so typical of the period. Hepplewhite writes of yet another type, a 'Commode Dressing Table,' that the serpentine fronted drawers are 'elegantly ornamented with inlaid or painted work, which is applied with great beauty and elegance to this piece of furniture.'

This inlaid or painted decoration, variations of festoons of husks and flowers and ribbons encircling a central oval design, is illustrated in three separate examples for 'tops of dressing tables and commodes.' Finally, Hepplewhite, like Shearer, illustrates 'Rudd's Table' or 'Reflecting Dressing Table', which he describes as 'the most complete dressing table made, possessing every convenience which can be wanted, or mechanism or ingenuity supply'. He adds that the table's name is derived from its reputed inventor, 'a once popular character' but who exactly Rudd was remains a mystery. It may possibly be the notorious courtesan, Mrs. Caroline Rudd, who was implicated (and later acquitted) in 1775 in a trial for forgery at the Old Bailey. The table, on four tapered legs, has two smaller side drawers which are made to swing out and are provided with mirrors on a quadrant so that a lady seated before it could view herself at any angle.

Thomas Sheraton's fame is based principally on *The Cabinet-Maker and Upholsterer's Drawing Book* which was published in parts between 1791 and 1794. This pattern book caught the last phase of the Adam style and gave Sheraton's name to the range of delicate and compact furniture which was fashionable about 1800 and bridged the passage between Adam's interpretation of Neo-Classicism and the more strictly archaeological interpretation of the Regency. More is known of Sheraton's career (1751–1806) than of Shearer's or Hepplewhite's but there is no evidence that he kept a shop or made furniture for, again, no piece of furniture made by him or under his direction has ever come to light. He eked out a precarious living as a drawing master. Yet no designs have excelled his in delicacy of form or ingenious arrangement (none more so than in dressing tables) or in the devising of furniture that could serve two or more purposes and yet, whenever possible, be light enough to be easily movable.

The dressing tables in the *Drawing Book* confirm the vogue for variety, from the simple table, knee-hole and chest of drawers to the occasional elaborate version. Hepplewhite's praise for Rudd's table is not echoed by Sheraton who takes some credit for its design to himself. In his description of a lady's knee-hole dressing table which has a pair of folding mirrors at the side, he claims that 'these side-glasses are an addition of my own, which I take to be an improvement; judging that, when they are finished in this manner, they will answer the end of a Rudd's table, at a less expense'. The *Drawing Book* illustrates two dressing chests, one with concave front, the other convex; both are also intended for writing, but while the former has only a slide, the latter has its top shallow drawer fitted with a movable writing flap and compartments for writing materials.

Of the more elaborate designs, one is for a lady's dressing commode and shows a bow fronted commode flanked by pedestal drawers; the other, even more complex, is a lady's cabinet dressing table. The latter, writes Sheraton, 'contains every requisite for a lady to dress at.' Knee-hole in form, bow fronted, it has a tambour below the central drawer and its small flanking drawers. Above are two small cupboards

Figure 12. Knee-hole dressing table, rosewood, with turned legs, c.1810.

with drawers and pigeon holes, and between these is an oval mirror with two more drawers below. On each side is a swing mirror of the 'Rudd' type already described. The central drawer of the knee-hole is fitted for washing; above it is a writing slide, while the right-hand drawer under the central mirror contains ink and sand. The rest of the small drawers in this section 'are intended to hold all the ornaments of dress, as rings, drops, etc'. This compact arrangement is made to appear more elaborate than it really is by the draperies and tassels which surround the table beneath the tambour. There is also drapery behind the central mirror and this 'may be real to suit that below, or it may only be painted in imitation of it'.

The knee-hole dressing table with central cupboard and flanking drawers, and the table with fitted drawer continued to enjoy great popularity *[figs.12, 13]*. Both types were supplied to Kew Palace in 1805 by the royal cabinet-maker, Charles Elliott, as the following extracts from the Lord Chamberlain's accounts show:

Figure 13. Knee-hole dressing table, semicircular, marquetry of hardwood and other woods, late 18th century.

'His Majesty's Bedroom. A best mahogany Dressing Table with drawers and a cupboard, folding top, glass to rise, on castors. £7. 2s.
Princess Elizabeth's Dressing Room. A handsome mahogany Dressing Table cross banded with satinwood, rising glass, scent bottles, tins for powers, a drawer with good lock and key, on brass castors. £10.18s.'[1]

While the interior arrangements of dressing tables became more complex the toilet-glasses which stood by or on them retained their simplicity *[fig.14]*. After its introduction about 1725 for furniture-making mahogany was increasingly used for glasses of this kind. For Chinese bedrooms, however, the frames were of soft wood and were carved and gilt, or japanned. Sometimes frames were draped in silk or velvet or similar materials to match the festooned dressing tables on which they stood. The best known example of this is Zoffany's painting of Queen Charlotte, wife of George III, seated at her dressing table in Buckingham House.

With the advent of Adam's Neo-Classical style in the 1760s toilet-glasses adopted oval and shield shaped frames, very similar in outline to the chair backs of the period, standing on box supports which were now single tiers of drawers. In mahogany or satinwood, or 'inlaid with coloured woods, or painted and varnished,' as Hepplewhite recommended in his *Guide*, these graceful pieces often had their uprights curved to match the shape of the glass. A simpler version, known as a 'skeleton glass', had a slender turned frame supported on claws *[fig.15]*.

The general vertical appearance of these glasses was influenced by the elaborate hair styles which reached England from France after the end of the Seven Years' War (1763). For some twenty years towering structures of powdered curls, both natural and false (considerable quantities of human hair were imported to help build up this 'Frenched hair') remained in fashion among wealthy women, to the delight of caricaturists *[pl.10]*. Men too were affected by the fashion. In the 1770s the Macaronis, the dandies of the time, wore enormous wigs and

1. Public Record Office. Lord Chamberlain's Accounts, 11/8 (1803–5).

Figure 14 (left). Dressing-glass, mahogany, on pillar and claws, c.1750.

Figure 15. 'Skeleton' toilet-glass, mahogany, c.1785.

long curls. These 'travelled young men who wear long curls and spying-glasses', as Horace Walpole described them, aped continental fashions in extremes of clothes and cosmetics which they had seen during their grand tours. The fashion for these high head-dresses, which could be positively dangerous for ladies when near lighted candles–there are records of fatalities–began to die out in the 1780s under the double influence of the French Revolution, which favoured simpler hair styles in contrast to the extravagant tastes of the *ancien régime,* and of the archaeological phase of Neo-Classicism, which encouraged flat and close hair styles based on the examples of classical antiquity.

Thus in the closing years of the century oval and shield shapes were replaced by oblong glasses swinging on turned or tapered uprights which were usually based on square or bow fronted stands with projecting corners. Bracket feet gave way to ivory or bone knobs with handles and escutcheons of the same materials. Mahogany or rosewood (the fashionable Regency wood), or occasionally satinwood, were principally used. For decoration, simple inlaid lines (stringing) or plain banding were adopted, for the long war with France, from 1793 to 1815, and the consequent heavy taxation, put expensive methods of decoration like carving and marquetry out of fashion.

The last quarter of the eighteenth century saw the advent of the cheval or horse dressing-glass after improved glass-making techniques led to the production of single plates up to ten feet in height. The obvious advantage of being able to view the whole person in a single mirror soon established this new form. The tall glasses stood on a four-legged frame (whence their name) and the glass was either tilted on swivel screws or was raised and lowered by means of lead weights within the uprights. Adjustable candle branches were often fixed to the uprights. Sheraton illustrates two distinct types of horse dressing-glasses in his *Drawing Book*. One is a tall glass which has a small toilet box fixed to each upright, one box including a comb-tray, the other a pin-cushion, among the small compartments. These boxes swing behind the glass when not in use. The other example has a smaller mirror, oval in shape and set horizontally on its frame; below it is a dressing drawer 'with convenience for writing as well as dressing' which, when closed, can be locked into the top rail above the glass. The lower parts of the supports are lyre shaped with brass strings, and a tray connects the supports above the feet.

The cheval glasses illustrated in George Smith's *Household Furniture* of 1808 have lost much of the graceful precision of the late eighteenth century examples. Anthemion cresting is found on the designs for glasses in the current classical taste, one of which has lion monopodia at the base of each upright. A design in Egyptian taste has griffin supports at each base and Egyptian heads surmount the uprights. Many Regency cheval glasses, however, used turned decoration to good effect. Figure 16 (p.49) illustrates a glass of about 1820 of ebony inlaid, with turned uprights and cross rails.

Plate 8. Pedestal dressing table in Neo-Classical taste, c.1775.

Plate 9. Dressing table, mahogany veneered with harewood,
c.1780; similar to design in Hepplewhite's *Guide* and
Sheraton's *Drawing Book (Appendix)*.

Plate 10. Caricature of women's coiffures by M. Darly, 1777.

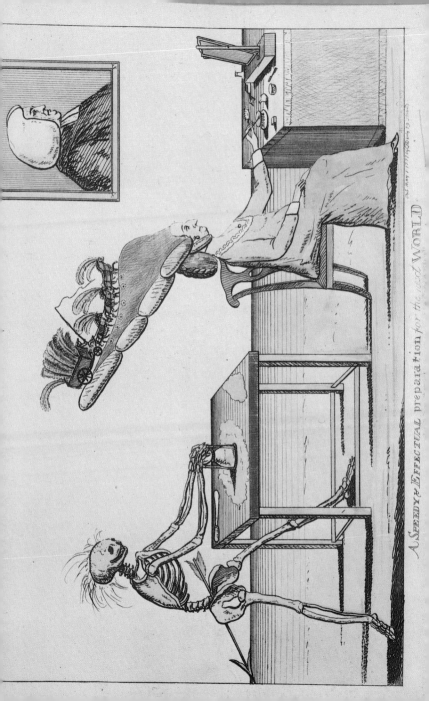

A SPEEDY & EFFECTUAL preparation for the next WORLD

Pub May 1 1777 by Bowles 13 Street

Plate 11. Wardrobe, mahogany, carved Rococo ornament; attributed to Giles Grendey, c.1750.

Plate 12. Wardrobe; chinoiserie details in green on white ground.
Made by Chippendale for David Garrick, c.1770.

Plate 13. Knee-hole dressing table designed by Owen Jones for
Eynsham Hall, Oxfordshire, c.1873.

Plate 14. Wardrobe designed by P. Webb and painted by E. Burne-Jones, made for William Morris, 1858–9.

Plate 15. Silver frame in Art Nouveau style by Liberty and Co, 1908.

Mahogany was an excellent material for wardrobes. Its wide planks for doors, on which its rich colour and figure show to great advantage, and its suitability for carving prompted increasing attention from leading cabinet-makers. These features are illustrated in plate 11, a wardrobe on stand, attributed on stylistic grounds to Giles Grendey of Clerkenwell, London. The doors have fielded (i.e. raised) panels, exploiting the figure of the wood. The rich carving of the stand, emphasised by the incised diaper background, and of the claw feet is in Rococo taste and suggests a date of about 1750. The flowing lines of the panels are broken at their centres. In contrast to the decoration of the stand there is delicate carved ornament on the cornice, at the sides and within the serpentine frame of the panels. Inside the wardrobe are adjustable shelves and, below, drawers made of cedar with which the whole interior is lined.

Figure 17 shows the type of wardrobe made about 1760

Figure 16 (left). Cheval dressing-glass, ebony inlaid, turned uprights and cross rails, c.1820.

Figure 17. Clothes press, carved mahogany, c.1760; a standard type for half a century.

which, with modifications in the mouldings, cornice and feet and in the decorative treatment dictated by changes in fashion, was to become standard in the second half of the century. This example, in mahogany, with four fielded panels on the doors, has carved fret decoration and is surmounted by a pierced Chinese fret. Chippendale illustrates a design of a wardrobe of this type in his *Director* and he is known to have made a number for clients. They were not expensive, for ten guineas was charged for one supplied to Mersham in 1767.

Naturally in other designs in the *Director* Chippendale gives full rein to Rococo forms. In the 1754 edition a 'commode clothes-press' has its lower stage of drawers (in two tiers, the upper with two short drawers, the lower with one long one) in bombé form on elaborately carved feet. Another design has serpentine doors and drawers and Chinese lattice work on its canted corners. There are surviving pieces based on each of these designs.

As japanning was such a favourite form of decoration for bedroom furniture many wardrobes were treated in this manner. The best known example is that supplied by Chippendale for the Chinese Bedroom at Nostell Priory, Yorkshire, in 1771. The Museum has fine examples of japanned wardrobes which were made by Chippendale's firm for the actor, David Garrick, for his villa at Hampton, Middlesex, about 1770. Plate 12 shows one of a pair of these wardrobes, of pine with chinoiserie details painted in dark green on a white ground. The general proportions and the mouldings are in Neo-Classical taste; classical paterae can be seen mingled with the chinoiserie decoration at the corners of the mouldings on the doors.

A wardrobe of a different kind from Garrick's villa is also of pine and has the same kind of green and white decoration, but in this case is in pure Neo-Classical style. The panels are of looking-glass. The drawer fronts of the lower stage are sham. This piece has special interest as it was originally a press bed which folded away inside the wardrobe the doors of which let down to support the bedding. The bed fittings have been removed, an alteration which has been made to many press beds, particularly in the early nineteenth century when J. C. Loudon, in his *Encyclopaedia of Cottage, Farm and Villa Architecture and Furniture,* first published in 1833, makes special mention of the practice.

Hepplewhite's *Guide* has several designs of wardrobes of standard type, of simple outlines stressing good proportions, with bracket or outward curving feet. Three tiers of drawers were normal, two smaller ones at the top, two longer ones below. The doors have selected figured mahogany and disclose the usual sliding shelves. Hepplewhite's text states that these wardrobes 'are usually made plain but of the best mahogany' *[fig.18].*

In the last quarter of the century it became customary to hang more clothes, especially ladies' dresses and as a result larger wardrobes were made, consisting of a standard piece flanked by recessed hanging cupboards. Sheraton's design for a wardrobe of this kind (in the *Appendix,* 1802, to his *Drawing Book* though the plate is dated 1793) is seen in figure 19. The text describes the upper central part as containing six or seven shelves of about six or six and a half inches deep, 'with green baize tacked to the inside of the front to cover the clothes with. The lower part consists of real drawers. The wings have each of them arms, to hang clothes on, made of beech, with a swivel in their centre, which slips on to an iron rod.' These 'arms' are like

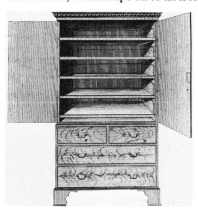

Figure 18. Design for a wardrobe from Hepplewhite's *Guide,* 1788.

51

Figure 19. Design for a wardrobe in the *Appendix* to Sheraton's *Drawing Book*.

modern coat and dress hangers. The whole wardrobe was made in four separate parts for the two wings and the upper and lower parts of the centre section could all be separated.

The late eighteenth century provides us with most surviving wig stands. Wigs have had such a long history – from the many known to have been worn by Elizabeth I to Pepys' many references to their great revival under Charles II and culminating in the full-bottomed wigs of Queen Anne's reign–that supports of some kind must have been made for them when they were not being worn. We can assume that surviving stands followed traditional forms, the simplest of which is the short turned stand, usually on a circular base, with a knob- or mushroom-shaped top for the wig. Travelling wig stands could be taken apart and packed flat. Double stands had two arms, each with its shaped top. More elaborate were the wig blocks which had a large hollow head, covered with leather, in which were kept the hair dressing equipment or small tools for the wigmakers. Bonnet stands were very similar to wig stands [fig.20].

Wigs required a special powder which was applied with powdering bellows or with a flexible tube (known from its shape as a 'carrot') capable of being directed at any angle. It was Pitt's war-time tax on wig powder which helped ultimately to end the wearing of wigs. The valet at his master's dressing table and the lady's maid at her mistress's were responsible for this powdering. They were also busy with curling irons. Sometimes negro servants, specially trained to dress hair, were in attendance. Below stairs the maids had been at work washing, starching and ironing clothes. In addition to smoothing irons, goffering irons were used to produce the ornamental plaiting for frills and for crimping starched materials. This work was carried out on ironing boards, usually hinged flaps with folding brackets, fixed to the wall. Clothes horses, light wooden frames, or folding types with two or three leaves, were other simple but essential pieces. The footmen in large households were responsible for cleaning boots and shoes as well as cleaning and brushing clothes, hats and gloves. For the last named glove stretchers (or 'wooden hands') were needed. When ready, boots and shoes were stacked on boot racks, the horizontal bars in the lower part of wardrobes.

Figure 20. Bonnet stand. Semicircular base with drawer at each end. Veneered with mahogany and other woods.

5 The Victorians and after

The extravagances of Georgian make-up were disappearing before the last George died. During Victoria's long reign (1837–1901) increased medical knowledge not only revealed the dangers in so many of the established cosmetics but went further by encouraging the cult of cleanliness. When John Wesley had written of cleanliness being next to godliness he was referring to dress; now it applied to the personal use of soap and water. The old soap tax was halved in 1833 and abolished in 1853 – an immense stimulus to the production of soap and, in consequence, perfumes. At the Great Exhibition in London in 1851, Class XXIX of exhibits (Miscellaneous Manufactures and Small Wares) included a considerable display of perfumes and soaps, among them eau-de-cologne, exhibited by Farina of Cologne, which was now to have a position of special esteem in English homes. The scope for cosmetics widened even more after 1851 when synthetic perfumes came on the market.

Cosmetics continued in use among women but with considerably more discretion. Cold cream, rouge and powder were normal, but not lip stick. For men as for women macassar oil was regarded as unrivalled for the hair and its use produced that universal feature of the Victorian interior, the antimacassar on sofas and chairs. Make-up achieved complete respectability when Mrs. Haweis published *The Art of Beauty* in 1878, for the author was the wife of a London vicar and was addressing mainly middle-class and especially younger women. Her very first page makes her aim clear: 'The culture of beauty is everywhere a legitimate art . . . it is not 'wicked' to take pains with oneself.' She adds later that 'an unnecessary amount of contempt and contumely has been cast on cosmetics' because paint had been considered to exhibit a certain showy vulgarity, yet 'it is generally a harmless, and, in some cases, a most necessary and decent practice'. By the end of the century, and certainly in the Edwardian era, ever greater freedom was achieved. Queen Alexandra used quite elaborate make-up and Lily Langtry, the reigning beauty and mistress of the Prince of Wales, allowed her photograph to be used to advertise Pears' soap.

In the world of furniture, after Georgian grace came Victorian comfort. Niceties of form were now secondary to the provision of ease. The Industrial Revolution–and Britain was the world's first industrialised society–was the universal provider. The railways brought the building materials to the new expanding suburbs. A place of one's own was no longer a dream; for the bulk of the population it was fast becoming a reality. Ever-increasing numbers of furniture firms, able to enlist the aid of more and more mechanical processes for more and more timbers coming from all parts of the world, turned out a greater quantity of furniture than had ever been seen before in England. The Yorkshire woollen mills provided good, abundant and cheap materials for the furnishings of the home. Springs made seating furniture ever more comfortable and ever more bulky. Comfort indeed was an accepted part of the Victorian creed. It was the reward for honest toil, properly due to those whose labour produced such a providential abundance of goods. 'All', wrote Loudon, 'from the highest to the lowest, are beginning to recognise their equal natural right of enjoyment.'

It would be impossible here to detail all the stylistic changes of Victoria's reign. In 1833 Loudon had described four current fashionable styles in furniture–the Grecian, Gothic, Elizabethan and Louis Quatorze. At the Great Exhibition of 1851 these had multiplied, with versions of the Renaissance and of the French *ancien régime*. Then after about 1870 came a whole series of revivals of the English styles of the eighteenth century which had hitherto been out of favour. At about the same time came inspiration from a new quarter, Japan, and the development of what is termed Anglo-Japanese furniture. By the end of the century we see the effects of reformers intent on reviving the highest standards of craftsmanship. The Arts and Crafts

Movement took root in the 1880s. In the last decade of the century appeared a completely new style, Art Nouveau.

In this medley of styles the task of identification is complicated by the widespread ignorance of art history which existed in the first half of Victoria's reign. Styles which were so readily interpreted were misunderstood. 'Elizabethan', for instance, included features which we recognise today as late Stuart; a favourite motif was the spiral turned leg or column which could be seen on the legs of dressing tables or on the uprights of toilet glasses. The cult of the Picturesque, the Romantic Movement, the reaction against two centuries of classical forms and decoration, the reaction, too, against the increasingly sordid features of industrialisation, all aroused a harkening back to the past. Early Victorian sentimentality was never far from a romantic medievalism which was nurtured by Scott's novels and Tennyson's poetry, by A. W. N. Pugin's glorification of the Gothic past and William Morris's veneration (not always, it must be added, pursued wholeheartedly) for traditional cottage joinery. A curious side effect of all this was the use of symbolic ornament on furniture, related to the function of the piece concerned and promoting association of ideas. This could go to absurd lengths, perhaps the most absurd example of all being found in Richard Brown's *The Rudiments of Drawing Cabinet and Upholstery Furniture,* published in 1820–much earlier, it can be noted, than one would normally suppose and an indication that much of what stands for Victorian innovation was clearly in being in the Georgian period. Brown, referring to bedroom furniture, suggests that decoration of a dressing table could be marquetry of scented flowers and 'running fig-leaves to denote the dress of our first parents'. For a cheval looking-glass he proposes a representation of 'the figure of Narcissus, who fell in love with his own image,' as this would 'show our folly in being too much in love with our own persons.' This romantic aura of the past was to linger for a long time. The architect, Robert Kerr (*The Gentleman's House,* 1864) describes the boudoir as 'the private sitting-room of the lady of the house. It is the Lady's Bower of olden time'.

Until about the time of the Great Exhibition (where the over-elaborate furniture was not typical of normal production) a multitude of pattern books, very much on the lines of those of the previous century, provide us with designs of bedroom furniture interpreting the current styles. Thereafter comes a change in the shape of firms' catalogues illustrating their furniture with drawings and later with photographs. Some catalogues were intended for well-to-do clients; others came from wholesalers, displaying goods which could be ordered by retailers in all parts of the country. A significant development was the growing number of firms specialising in bedroom furniture and looking-glasses.

Dressing tables in the early pattern books are in general of two main types: the table on four legs or on standards (end supports) and cross stretcher, and the knee-hole pedestal. These are seen, for example, in the designs of Thomas King, a prolific publisher of pattern books between 1829 and about 1840. There is no doubt of his appeal to a wide public, though very little is known about him, for his best-known work, *The Modern Style of Cabinet Work Exemplified*, was re-issued unaltered (except for additional plates) as late as 1862–a tribute, incidentally, to the strong conservatism of early Victorian taste. King's tables conform to the Elizabethan style by adopting spiral turning, and to the Louis Quatorze by having cabriole legs and curved supports. This was the usual procedure of the time: styles were interpreted by merely adding the appropriate trimmings to standard pieces of furniture. In other designs King reveals Victorian innovations by increasing heaviness and rotundity of form. A typical example in *The Modern Style* is a dressing table with four thick round legs standing on a plinth which is curved in front for the sitter's feet. Two long narrow drawers run from front to back at each end of the table top and between them, at the back, stands the mirror.

For the rest of the century firms rang the changes on these two main types, adopted, for instance, by Shoolbreds of Tottenham Court Road, one of London's principal areas for high-class, ready-made furniture. Their catalogues from the

1870s show these types in bedroom suites in, among others, Japanese, Adam, Stuart and Early English styles. One modification, however, can be seen; sometimes a tall looking-glass, of cheval glass proportions, stands between two sets of drawers. The Victoria and Albert Museum has a fine example of the traditional knee-hole pedestal dressing table of about 1873. This was designed by the prominent architect-designer, Owen Jones *[pl.13]*. The kind of furniture which was advocated by devotees of a simpler Gothic style is in Charles L. Eastlake's *Hints on Household Taste*, 1868. Eastlake, whose work had a considerable following in America, deplored the current tendency in furniture 'to run into curves', and saw reform in simple, cheap, rectangular Gothic pieces. A dressing table illustrated by him was made by Jackson and Graham of Oxford Street, London, one of the most important furniture firms of the 1860s and 1870s. Simplicity is also evident in the bedroom suite by Holland and Sons, of Mount Street *[fig.21]*, illustrated in Robert W. Edis's *Decoration and Furniture of Town Houses*, 1881. As seen here, it was now usual to stand the toilet glass on

Figure 21. Bedroom furniture by Holland and Sons, from R. Edis's *Decoration and Furniture of Town Houses*, 1881.

the table top between nests of drawers or small cupboards. Edis writes that 'the general designs are well adapted for cheap bedroom furniture in light stained or lacquer-painted wood'.

An important reason for the growing simplicity of bedroom furniture towards the end of the century was hygiene. Dust and dirt were enemies to be tackled at all costs. Furniture, and particularly that in the bedroom, must wherever possible be easily movable so that the whole room could be thoroughly and quickly cleaned. Such is the theme of Lady Barker's *The Bedroom and the Boudoir*, 1878, one of the series of small books published in the late 1870s under the umbrella title of *Art at Home*, describing all the modern improvements in furniture and furnishings, for 'the cultivated middle-class able to enjoy leisure, refinement and luxury in moderation'.[1] Lady Barker strongly favoured what she called the 'ordinary' dressing table which had a 'scoop out of the middle' for the knees, a couple of drawers each side, and a 'large toilet glass of equally uncompromising utility and convenience'.

Both the free-standing toilet-glass and the cheval glass retained their appeal. They became cheaper as glass-making techniques continued to improve. Early Victorian toilet glasses usually stood on solid curved plinths with four small feet and had their uprights turned or curved to conform with current styles. Even after fashionable firms incorporated swing glasses at the back of dressing tables between supporting small drawers or cupboards, the free-standing glasses were produced in considerable numbers for smaller homes. Specialists in this line were C. and R. Light of Curtain Road, Shoreditch, the area of East London associated with the mass production of cheaper furniture. This firm were one of the largest wholesale businesses in the country at the turn of the century and their looking-glasses must have reached an extensive market.

In her advocacy of easily movable furniture Lady Barker had the large Victorian wardrobe in mind, for she comments tartly

1. Rhoda and Agnes Garrett, *Suggestions for House Decoration (Art at Home)*, 1876.

that few articles of furniture had had more lavish pains bestowed upon them. These wardrobes were of the break-front type–central cupboard and two flanking cupboards–which were fashionable well before 1800. Many versions of this type appear in pattern books before 1850. Some reached monumental proportions as was already forecast in George Smith's *The Cabinet-Makers and Upholsterers' Guide*, published 1828, for this includes a design in which the central cupboard is linked to the side ones by additional sets of drawers. Inevitably the surfaces of large wardrobes provided ample scope for decoration in all the prevailing styles. One innovation which appeared before 1850 was a full-length looking-glass fitted to the central door.

It is noticeable, however, that after 1850 commercial production was concerned also with smaller wardrobes for the medium-priced market. One of the first firms to issue catalogues were William Smee and Sons of Finsbury Pavement, London, who were both wholesalers and retailers. Their early catalogue, of about 1850–55, includes, among larger varieties, examples of the standard late Georgian wardrobe of a cupboard standing on a chest of drawers. As can be expected, Lady Barker solved her problem by wholehearted support of smaller wardrobes, the best kind of all being in what she calls 'the essentially modern style'. She illustrates a number which are cupboards, preferably with one door only, with two or three drawers below. She dislikes any attempt at the Gothic, medieval or indeed any other style. Plain pine, varnished or ebonised (the latter was a fashionable treatment at that time), or even deal would suffice. Corner wardrobes are also warmly recommended.

Wardrobes give us excellent examples of some of the decorative fashions of the second half of the century. Plate 14 illustrates the painted decoration inspired by William Morris. This wardrobe, designed by Philip Webb, later the chief furniture designer of Morris and Company, founded in 1861, and painted by Morris's artist friend, Edward Burne-Jones, with a scene from Chaucer's *Prioress's Tale*, was made about 1858–9 as a wedding present for Morris. It is an early example of the more elaborate 'state' furniture which Morris's firm was later to make for wealthy clients in contrast to the cheaper 'workaday' pieces. A design for a wardrobe by William Burges shows the boarded construction and long hinges which were characteristic of Burges's reformed Gothic furniture of the 1860s, and characteristic, too, of Eastlake's designs. An oak and pine wardrobe in the Egyptian style of about 1878–80 is painted with hieroglyphics and other Egyptian motifs and has four fluted Egyptian columns. Liberty's of Regent Street were largely responsible for the fashion for Egyptian and oriental furniture and the furnishings as they were also for Art Nouveau furniture *[pl.15 and fig.22]*.

If the Edwardian era left behind it lingering doubts that make-up was still associated with high-society ladies, actresses and the demi-monde, these were soon to be dispelled. The freedom given to women by two world wars, their increased

Figure 22. Dressing table by C. R. MacKintosh, 1916.

spending power, extended in recent times to teen-agers, and the vastly increased output of wholesome cosmetics have all brought the art of make-up to every Englishwoman. Mass advertising has cleverly exploited this market. Both the cinema screen and television have produced fashionable faces and the means to imitate them have been readily available. The results are there for all to see.

As for furniture, the dressing table, toilet-glass and wardrobe, developed, as we have seen, over the centuries, still retain their place. Modern designers are giving them the same close attention as did their predecessors of the Stuart period. How well they have succeeded with modern resources and materials is a matter for the reader's judgement. We conclude with an example of the work of one of the greatest English designers of the twentieth century [fig.23].

Figure 23. Wardrobe, macassar ebony, designed by Ambrose Heal, c.1930.

Bibliography

Angeloglou, M. *A. History of Make-up.* 1970.

Aslin, E. *19th. Century English Furniture.* 1962.

Baker, Hollis, S. *Furniture in the Ancient World.* 1966.

Barker, Lady. *The Bedroom and the Boudoir.* 1878.

Dictionary of Victorian Furniture Designs. 1977.

Edis, R.W. *Decoration and Furniture of Town Houses.* 1881.

Edwards, R. *The Shorter Dictionary of English Furniture.* 1964.

Fowler, J. and Cornforth, J. *English Decoration in the 18th. Century.*
    1974.

Garrett, R. and A. *Suggestions for House Decoration.* 1876.

Giedion, S. *Mechanization Takes Command.* 1955.

Harris, J. *Regency Furniture Designs.* 1961.

Haweis, Mrs. H.R. *The Art of Beauty.* 1878.

Hayward, H. (ed.). *World Furniture.* 1963.

Jervis, S. *Victorian Furniture.* 1968.

Liversidge, J. *Furniture in Roman Britain.* 1955.

Loudon, J.C. *Encyclopaedia of Cottage, Farm and Villa Architecture
    and Furniture, 1833 and later.*

Williams, N. *Powder and Paint.* 1957.

Wills, G. *English Looking-Glasses.* 1965.

General There are various editions of the diaries of John Evelyn
and Samuel Pepys, and reprints (e.g. Tiranti and Dover
Publications) of the pattern books of Chippendale, Hepplewhite and
Sheraton. Tiranti have also reprinted Stalker and Parker's *Treatise
of Japanning.*

Index

Printed in England for Her Majesty's Stationery Office by Balding + Mansell, Wisbech
Dd. 587528 K80